DEDICATION

This book is dedicated to everyone who cherishes their present relationship and to those who are trying to prepare themselves to never let the right one get away again.

SPECIAL THANKS

To **LuAnne** for the sacrifices made for me to finish this project

To **Byrdology** for your belief and your brilliance

To my editor, **Seth Libby**

To **Maurice Downing** and **MoDesignz** for making me look so much better than I am.

HAPPIER ENDINGS

HOW TO GUARD YOUR RELATIONSHIP'S FUTURE

INTRODUCTION

Love may never die, but relationships do end. Some need to, but many relationships that end could have and should have lasted. The regret we feel after leaving a good relationship can be quite a blow to the psyche and the emotions. Do you have a "the one that got away" story or a "I wish I hadn't blown that one" memory? Wouldn't it be great if the final commentary on those relationships had been, "...And they lived happily ever after"?

I think it would be fantastic if every time two good people got married they stayed together until natural death parted them. But we know that is not the case. Relationships end, even good relationships, and some of them badly.

Relationships are a collection of interactions, experiences, and moments in time where each individual chooses to behave in a way that either further secures the couple's connection or causes the stability of their union to blow up or slowly crumble over time. In each encounter with our partner, we have the ability to choose to have a happier relationship. If you want your relationship to last forever, you will have to consistently protect its future. Your happy ending has to be cultivated and protected on a daily basis.

In this book, we'll explore our interpersonal habits and how they affect the success of our love lives. This book offers insight and wisdom to those who wish to have more satisfying romantic alliances. The goal is to help you to get to the point where the epitaph of your relationship is, "... And they lived happily ever after."

I've said in previous books and talks that a relationship is work. Real, happily-ever-after love is work. When it is right, it is a joy and a pleasure, but you must work to make and keep it what it should be. Daily, you have to show up, clock in, execute your tasks, and perform your duties. Every day, you have to get to work. That does not sound romantic, does it? The fact is, though, making anything a success takes a lot of work. Many of the ingredients necessary to make your favorite meal don't sound particularly delicious on their own. Yet, the right cook takes those ingredients, works his or her magic, and the results make your taste buds very happy.

The work required to make your relationship last is simple to describe but hard to achieve. To have relationship success, we must first do our best to create an appropriate context in which the union can thrive, while also effectively managing the variables we cannot control. Often, relationships end and end badly because individuals have initiated it under terrible circumstances or placed it in a bad situation that is not conducive for their pursuit of happiness. The conditions matter. Secondly, if we want to have happier endings, we have to do more than say the right words, we have to develop the character necessary to guide our actions and behavior properly. Actions do speak louder than words. Or, as my late Granny use to say, "You have to act right." When it comes to your relationship, there is no substitute for good character.

In Happier Endings, we will explore 18 real-life relationship scenarios. Each of these will describe a condition, action, behavior, or motive that affects the health of your relationship. Increasing your awareness and understanding of these areas is paramount to guarding your relationship's future. When you properly manage them, they will help protect the happy ending for which you hope and desire. Mismanaging them can have the effect of either dynamite or termites, instant explosion or damage you do not see until things start crumbling. Obviously, neither is desirable, and both can be fatal to your relationship, which is why you have to be on guard daily to protect the future.

1

Deep End

One summer, my nephews and I were swimming in my dad's pool. Let me be more accurate. Tahron and Tehriq were swimming. I was playing in the water because I cannot swim. We were having a great time splashing around and playing catch with a football. Because they were swimmers, the boys explored the full depth of the pool as they caught and missed passes. I stayed at the shallow end of the pool, venturing no further than the 5-foot mark. Then, I missed a pass, a bad throw by one of the adolescents. The ball sailed to the deepest end of the pool, where I could not retrieve it. One of my nephews had to go and get the ball. Because I don't swim, I can only play in the shallow end of the water. Anything at the deep end of the pool is simply out of my reach.

When a relationship wades into the deep end, emotional capital has been invested, and there are real feelings involved. Once out of shallow waters, there are now expectations about the present and future of the relationship. Some people try to stay away from the deep end because, consciously or subconsciously, they are not ready for the vulnerability that comes with such an involved relationship.

They won't admit they are in love. They try to say, "It's cool, but I can take it or leave it." But that is no longer true. This is different. Things have gone past just having good times with good company, and it is time to admit it. They have hit the deep end, and they've got to start swimming.

Deep-end relationships are long-term, exclusive, and require you to be fully invested. They are not casual or transactional. They are not for the moment, for the night, or for the time being. When you enter the deep end in the relationship, you hope that it will last for the rest of your life. The deep end is not for everyone though. Some people are not in the market for a deep-end relationship, and that's okay. When you know that you aren't looking for anything too deep, make it known to those you date and manage the relationship accordingly. Communicate your intent. Set your boundaries. Operate the relationship within those parameters, and periodically evaluate your thoughts, feelings, and actions. Communicate, operate, and evaluate.

Here is a warning, though. You cannot control whether or not your partner wanders or launches out into the deep. Just because you do not want to enter the deep end of a relationship does not mean the person you are dating will not. When one person is in deep and the other person is still in shallow water, the imbalance will throw off the symmetry of the relationship and also the emotional equilibrium of the individual at the deep end. That is a difficult inequality to manage. No one wants to be in the deep end alone. That's not a great place to be.

Why wouldn't an individual want to go to the deep end,

especially if they are enjoying their company in the relationship pool? The answer may be in their lack of ability. When I was in the pool with my nephews, I did not go into the deep end of the pool because I cannot swim. After 50+ years of life I have never learned. I tried to, but because I am unable to relax in water, I never actively pursued lessons. When it comes to swimming pools or natural bodies of water, I confine myself to the 5-foot mark. I am 6'1", so it works for me. I would love to have fun at the deep end, but I can't. I do not have the requisite skills to function at that level. I cannot swim. I wanted to go there. The deep end offers opportunities and possibilities that are not available at the shallow end of the pool. But what is fun for my nephews would be dangerous even lethal for me. I do not have the skills, so I have to stay within the parameters of my abilities. The 5-foot mark is my limit. People fail at deep-end relationships because they don't have the proper skills and abilities. For that reason, some people intentionally remain in shallow-end partnerships. There are new levels of trust and vulnerability when you take the relationship to a deeper level. To manage these new responsibilities, successful serious relationships require romantic partners to have good communication and conflict resolution skills. When you don't have the requisite skills and abilities, you cannot go deep.

Skills and abilities have to be coupled with personal character. Some individuals are too shallow to ever allow themselves to reach the deep end of a relationship. Their romantic liaisons are transactional and a matter of utility. They date only to fulfill specific companionship, sexual, or esteem needs. For them, every amorous relationship is consciously or subconsciously meant to be temporary from the outset. They plan to stay in water they can stand up in and easily get out of if desired. Their relationships are meant to be superficial. They know what they want (or maybe they don't, which can be worse). They also know how much of themselves they are prepared to invest in whomever they are dating. Exclusivity may or may not be their aim, but they are not presently looking for "happily ever after."

If you are dating, please know there are people out there who cannot "swim." They don't have the necessary abilities to be in a deep-end relationship. They may have great potential, if only they would "get themselves together," but they aren't currently together. Please consider the following before you decide to take someone on as a project:

1. For most, it takes time to learn to swim
2. You cannot teach those who will not learn.
3. The relationship swim coach does not always end up being the synchronized swimming partner.

Those who enter and enjoy deep-end relationships are prepared with the proper relationship skills and traits that are required. They possess the selflessness, humility, patience, kindness, honor, respect, effective communication and conflict resolution skills, and the rest of the abilities needed to maneuver at the deep end. Some people wander into the deep end by accident. That can have some unfortunate outcomes. But if you are ready, there is a lot more enjoyment and many additional possibilities for exhilaration at the deep end. If you decide to go there or be taken there, just make sure you are ready to start swimming.

2

My End – Your End

My wife and I have been working on remodeling our bedroom. We painted the walls, had new carpet installed, and replaced our old bed, complete with a new bedspread and accent pillows. New bedroom furniture is coming soon. The finishing touch will be new window treatments. We have had to move things out of our bedroom and move things into it. Out with the old, and in with the new. All of the bedrooms in our house are on the second level. There are 17 steps between the first level and the second. How do I know? I counted them when we first moved into the house. I knew that I would have to carry things up and down those stairs often without the ability to see, so I counted them for my own safety. During this remodeling project, we have both taken things up and down those 17 stairs on our own. Some of the heavier items required both of us to share the load. We have been up and down those 17 steps, carrying headboards, mattresses, and furniture, my wife on one end and me on the other.

Every relationship has two ends, and both of them have to be bolstered. As Marvin Gaye and Kim Weston sang, "It takes two, baby," or as the classic Rob Base and DJ E-Z Rock track says, "It's takes two to make a thing go right. It takes two to make it out of sight." With the exception of cases where there has been a debilitating injury or illness, each individual is expected to do his or her equal part to make things go right and make the relationship work. Relationships are not meant to be one-sided. They require both parties to hold up their end.

We've all seen couples with the appearance of joy and contentment, where suddenly, sometimes in a single conversation, it becomes clear that one of them is actually unsatisfied and disheartened by their relationship. Their needs and desires are being ignored, while they themselves are being a good mate. They are distraught and emotionally exhausted because they cannot seem to please and satisfy their partner, no matter what they do. What an awful position to be in.

If you are in such a predicament, you have my sympathy and my prayers, but let me be clear regarding the subject of personal happiness. You are not obligated to make another person happy. Happiness truly is an inside job. In your relationship pursuits, find a happy person and make them happier. If your partner is a happy person, making them happier is simply a matter of holding up your end of the relationship. If your partner is an unhappy person, no amount of lifting on your end is going to lift them up.

Your end is the sum total of the relationship needs you have to fulfill and the expectations you have to meet. When I speak of needs, I am particularly focused on what I call dominant needs. Dominant needs are the interpersonal relationship requirements that people have that are unequivocal. They differ from person to person. For example, effective conflict resolution devoid of excessive quarreling is a dominant need of mine. A physically active spouse could be a dominant need. If you have ever seen a FarmersOnly.com commercial, you see that farmer's need for a woman who loves the great outdoors. Everyone has their own dominant needs. Regardless of who the partner or potential mate is, dominant needs are non-negotiable. They are must haves. Most people have three to five dominant needs. In my opinion, anything over five is not primary but secondary and is or should be negotiable.

Here is a list of needs we all have. Each of us has to decide which are dominant.

1. Physical Needs – Does your partner need to look a certain way?
2. Social Needs – What are your preferences relating to your social life?
3. Intellectual Needs – What is the intersecting point of intellectual compatibility?
4. Spiritual needs – How important is it for you to share in your spiritual, religious life?
5. Sexual Needs – What are your desires relative to frequency, experience, and the execution of your sex life?
6. Familial Needs – How large a family do you desire? How will your extended family be interwoven into your romantic life?

This is not the complete list. Your needs can come in any

of those categories, or they can be something completely different. The point is, your most dominant needs have to be met in order for the relationship to exist at all.

It takes keen self-awareness to know what one's dominant needs are and not to confuse them with secondary needs, regardless of how prominent the less important need seems to be at the time. For instance, is a definitive feeling about family (lots of kids or none) really a dominant need for you, or do you feel you are more open to change on that later? Do you really require a certain level of intellect, or can you see yourself happy with someone much smarter or much less smart than you? In order to be fair and reasonable, we can only place but so many demands on our mate. There has to be a limit. It is wise for us to ensure that our mate is aware and prepared to meet our dominant needs and for that to be foundational. When deciding on a mate, you can never lose sight of what is most important to you. If you do, somewhere down the line, your soul will remind you that something is missing because you traded a core need for the satisfaction of a surface desire. If you make a poor request of your partner, and then blame them for your discontentment, you have hampered your and your partner's ability to fully enjoy the relationship. Dominant needs always matter.

Your expectations are what you anticipate occurring in your relationship. Expectations are about how you will do life together. To differentiate, your needs are those things you desire that are deemed a necessity. They are similar to expectations, but in reality, they are the soil from which expectations sprout and grow. For example, it may be necessary that your partner is in a certain age range, have a certain level of spiritual commitment, or have a certain intellectual prowess. These needs will make it possible for them to meet your expectations as the relationship evolves.

Like needs, the expectations one has in a relationship are usually categorical. Ask yourself what you want from your partner in the major categories of interpersonal interaction and relationship life. Although the list can be much more exhaustive, some of the major categories of interpersonal interaction and relationship life are as follows:

1. Time and attention
2. Communication
3. Affection and sex
4. Money and finances
5. Domestic duties
6. Children and family
7. Spirituality and religious practices

What are your expectations in the above areas? As with your needs, you should not expect to receive what you have not communicated as an expectation. There should be no assumptions in this area. Your partner should know your expectations are so he or she can operate with the assurance that he or she can meet them. Unmet expectations are seeds of disappointment and potential conflict. Ironically, and unfortunately, it is possible to be in love with someone who does not meet your relationship expectations. Sometimes, we decide to love people based on their most positive traits and not necessarily on how they fulfill our most important desires regarding how we want to live or the way we want to be treated.

In order to improve the chances you will be treated the way you want to be treated in your relationship, you need to be clear on your own needs and expectations. To provide that clarity, you have to be able to see the difference between a need and an expectation, and then to decide what falls into each category, and what can be left out.

As a practice, needs and expectations should be known, communicated, and agreed upon. As I mentioned above, unknown needs and expectations will most likely go unmet. That means you need to participate in a little introspection. It is important to know what your needs and expectations are, so you can communicate them to your partner. Only then can you come to an agreement that your mate has the capacity and the willingness to meet and fulfill them.

Capacity and willingness are connected yet distinct. In my book, What You Say When You Say "I Do", I surmised that one of the primary purposes of dating is information gathering. An understanding of the capacity of a mate or potential partner is vital information that should be gathered. No matter what we want them to be or what they have the potential to become, at present, people are who they are and no more. Within the confines of a love relationship, it is unfair to demand more of a person than they are capable. It is also terrible to promise more than you are able to deliver. Capacity is a crucial factor when it comes to needs being met and expectations being fulfilled. People cannot give what they do not have. Each partner has to agree they are able and also willing to fulfill their mate's desires. You cannot force a person to hold up their end. He or she has to want to.

That's why communication is so important upfront. If you are honest about what you need and expect from your relationship, you can get an honest answer about your partner's capacity. If they have the capacity, and they show the willingness, you have a far easier road ahead to that happier ever after.

3

Front End – Back End

There are numerous factors that determine how a relationship ends up. Will there be happy ending or a sad one? Will the relationship abruptly and unnecessarily end, or will it run its complete course? Will it be fortifying or debilitating to each individual? Will the epitaph be, "It was good while it lasted," or, "That was a big mistake," or will both partners declare, "That was the best thing that has ever happened to me"? No one can completely predict the future of a relationship, and no one factor will completely determine a relationship's fate. All relationships have some level of risk. The risk you take to open your arms, your heart, and your life to someone cannot be totally eliminated, but one factor in particular can mitigate a lot of that risk: a solid foundation.

In the Bible, there is a story of two men who are each building a house. The men choose differing materials as the foundation for their respective structures. One uses solid rock; the other uses an alloyed material. By using the alloyed material, the builder is able to lay the foundation much quicker than his counterpart and, consequently, gets his house finished faster. A little later, the gentleman who chose solid rock for his foundation eventually finishes his home as well. Both men are seemingly pleased with their individual final products. As fate would have it, though, a storm with high winds and heavy rain hits the area. Both structures sustain damage, but the house built on the rock is able to withstand the storm without catastrophic damage. The other house is destroyed; it is a complete loss. The loss is attributed to the fact the foundation made with the alloyed material was not strong enough for the house to weather the storm.

Just as in home building, what comprises the foundation of a relationship is paramount. All relationships will encounter potentially destructive storms that will test what the relationship is made of. If the foundation is not solid, the damage can be cataclysmic. The front end of the relationship is where you build the foundation upon which everything else will be constructed. If the foundation isn't strong and solid, the future of the relationship is perpetually at risk. If you do not make the right investments on the front end of your relationship, you may pay a price on the back end. As a matter of fact, you could begin to experience negative consequences soon after the front-end period is over. That being said, it isn't always the easiest thing to do the front-end work right up front. It takes a great deal of discipline to properly manage the early stages of a relationship.

Let's admit it. The beginning period of new relationships is so much fun: the excitement, the intrigue, the constant affirmation of your esteem. There is nothing like the discovery stage. Conversations flow effortlessly. You seem to have so much in common. The jokes are funny, or at least cute. The life stories are interesting, or at least seem to be. Both parties bring their "A" game and put their best forward. Both people are oh-so-impressed and enthralled with each other. The vibe and the energy are amazing. The lunches, dinners, movies, and walks on the beach or in the park are so enjoyable. There are the text messages, cards, and gifts, and for the unsanctified, the thrill of unfamiliar sex with a new person you're really excited about. All of these things add up to a full course sensory meal that includes dessert. You just want the feeling to continue. To keep it going, you zero in on everything you like and pay no real attention to anything else. You make an assessment and draw the conclusion that the relationship works because you want it to work. Some even go so far as saying that they may have finally found their soulmate. We can get so caught up in the fun, we don't do the work of real research and evaluation.

It's hard to pull back in that exuberant moment and remember that one of the primary goals of dating is to gather the pertinent information to lay a proper foundation for the long-term health and viability of the relationship. Getting beyond the great dates and incredible conversations, the first thing you should ascertain on the front end is who the person really is. What is their temperament? What is their view of gender roles? What are their dreams and goals? What is their worldview? Are they kind and loving in general, or just to you? How do they handle pressure? The list goes on.

You should also evaluate who you are within the context of your interaction with this person. Are you confident and comfortable to be your complete self with them? Are you a great version of yourself when you are together? Do they bring the best out of you or trigger the worst?

In essence, you are trying to home in on a very basic, central question: are the two of you a good match? There can be two great individuals who do not make a great match. How well do you really fit? People who match well together complement and when necessary supplement each other without either feeling a sense of loss or unnatural sacrifice. This sort of information helps you lay the proper foundation for your relationship and should happen on the front end, right in the midst of the heady early days of your dating.

To many of you, this sounds like work. It is. While you are enjoying the beauty and excitement of the early stage of a relationship, you have to do your front-end work. Clean your lens, so you can see clearly. Filter your emotions, so you do not play games with your own head. Remember: when people show you who they really are, believe them. Distill any negative predispositions. You don't want to engage in romance sabotage. Take the necessary calculated risks during conversations, so you can get honest answers to good questions. Listen to the assessments and perceptions of other mature, trustworthy people concerning your new partner. And by all means, take your time. What is the rush? The stories of people meeting, falling in love at first sight, getting married three months later, and living happily ever after are beautiful. And they are real. They are just not prevalent. Open your ears, and you'll hear about the "blinded by love" heartbreak stories far more frequently. Take your time and lay a good foundation. Do your front-end work, so that nothing bites you unnecessarily in the butt on the back end.

4

End Game

As a child, I remember watching family sitcoms on television. There would usually be an episode in the series where a young man would have to meet his date's father. The young lady would still be getting ready, and you could see the awkward tension between the dad and the date. The young man would sit obviously nervous and possibly frightened, but he would eventually have to answer the question, "What are your intentions with my daughter?" As an adult, I saw this commonly portrayed scenario featured in a not-quite-so-family-friendly movie. Who can forget Will Smith and Martin Lawrence in the boyfriend at the door scene in Bad Boys 2? They took that young man through the ringer. There was a significant amount of profanity, but it was and is hilarious. (Pray for me, please.) Even if you have not seen the movie, you are aware of the type situation I'm describing. Whether it is rated G or rated R, the incident where the protective and often overprotective man asks a nervous suitor about his intentions concerning a young lady is a common one in television, cinema, and real homes across the world.

Things have changed quite a bit from the 80's, 90's, and

even the early 2000's. These days, it is not the protective father or brother asking a clarifying question. It is the dating individual themselves who are trying to decipher the intent of the person in which they are sharing consistent romantic time and space. People are asking questions such as, "What are we?" "What are we doing?" "Where are we going with this?" "Who am I to you?" "Why did you introduce me as your friend?" There is a term for such questions. It is called "defining the relationship," or DTR. The answer to DTR questions makes plain what is going on with said romance. When a person asks, "What's up with us," they are attempting to ascertain what the end game is for the romantic interaction.

I, for one, have always been curious about why people invest so much time, energy, and effort, while giving so much of themselves, before asking questions that clarify the relationship's end game. Why do so many languish in such undesirable ambiguity? They allow someone into the inner sanctum of their being, emotionally, psychologically, and physically, without any clear understanding of that someone's intent. They give of themselves, their resources, and their time—which is the most priceless resource we all have—without discussing what the end game is. Studies show that some people find it difficult to ask DTR questions and have the necessary relationship definition conversations. In many cases, they are afraid to upset the apple cart and choose to just leave well enough alone. They do not want to jeopardize what they have by asking questions about the long-term future, especially since there are those who do not like answering such questions.

I once saw a comedy sketch where a female asked her "friend," "What are we doing?" His response was, "We're eating good, going to movies, and having sex. That's what we are doing." Unfortunately, his statement accurately describes what many people call dating in today's culture. I have talked to individuals who manage their relationships totally in the now. They prefer to keep things undefined with no labels and would rather dawdle in relationship ambiguity. They have their reasons. Some do it out of fear, others out of a need to keep control of their lives and have an uncomplicated exit if necessary. Still others remain vague because they are aware that they and their partner have differing desires relative to the future. So, they manipulate the relationship with ambiguity in order not to reveal real intentions.

Allow me to assist you to clear away some of the fog that the lack of DTR answers can create. There are only a few answers to the "What are we doing" question. People engage in romantic relationships for one of the following reasons:

1. They just want to enjoy themselves and have fun. There is no end game.
2. The end game is to affirm themselves and stroke their ego.
3. The end game is companionship.
4. The end game is sex.
5. The end game is financial assistance.
6. The end game is exclusivity without marriage.
7. The end game is marriage.

There may be others, but these are the most prominent ones. I mentioned earlier that some people don't like having the DTR discussion because they know that their intent differs from their partner's. Take a good look at the list. Can you see how unsafe incongruence with your mate would be? Are there any good combinations of the seven reasons? How about 1 and 7? What about 2 and 6 or 3 and 5? Would 4 and 6 work? Unfortunately, many people are settling for some combination of 1, 3, 4, and 5: recreation and entertainment, coupled with companionship and sex, with some occasional (or consistent) financial assistance. If that is not enough for you, or it goes against your moral code or Christian ethics, you are going to need to find the courage to call for a day of reckoning and have that clarifying conversation.

Here is my counsel to those who prefer to be ambiguous in their relationships. Be honest. Operate with personal integrity, and do not waste people's time. Articulate your intentions and let people decide if they want to engage with you or not.

Here, too, are a few words of caution to those who do not want to rock the boat and lose what you have by asking too many questions about the end game. Ambiguity is a risk. Does it ever pay off? Sure, it does, but too often it does not. You vastly increase the risk of a bad ending by trying to leave well enough alone. Moreover, you deserve the answers you desire. You also deserve a person that wants to operate in the light of known intentions, a person who wants you to be clear and secure. Do not base your relationship on assumptions, incorrect conclusions, or a fallacy. Operate with full knowledge of what is going on. Do not just go along for the ride when you do not know where it ends.

5

A Means to an End

As said in the previous chapter, there are those who like to operate in relationship ambiguity because they are more comfortable in undefined romantic space. Yet, there are some who are well aware of their desired end game but choose to be vague because their true intent is less than honorable. I want to take a moment to focus in on this group of dishonorable lotharios.

I once saw a movie scene that I actually also saw play out in real life. I will tell you about the movie in order to protect the innocent. A couple was having a heated argument. They were breaking up. The female said some very terse words. The male responded, "It's ok. All you were for was sex anyway." She then responded, "Well, trust me, you won't have the pleasure ever again." I once heard a group of women talking. It was one of those times as a child I got stuck with my mom at the laundromat. You know the conversations that women can have while waiting on loads of clothes to watch and dry. One of them said, "I think it is time for me to find a man. I need someone to help me with these bills." One of the ladies responded, "Girl, I know what you mean." As a former pastor, I've watched "ministry marriages" begin and end or last until death all the while killing the souls of the individuals as they pretend to be happy for the good of appearance and public consumption. These relationships in many cases were void of true love and compatibility. Being married was needed to qualify for ministry elevation and opportunity. (For the record, I am so glad there has been a cultural shift away from this unwritten requirement. It is saving many from bad relationships.)

Each of the scenarios previously described are relationships that were utility and transactional in nature. The relationship itself was not the end game. The relationship was a means to an end. How awful it must be to be wanted not for who you are but for what hooking up with you can achieve or facilitate. There are certainly cases when a transactional alliance is agreed upon, and there are mutually accepted benefits. These are not real relationships but arrangements that provide advantages to both parties. While not optimal, or in many cases virtuous, at least they are mutually beneficial. However, these accepted transactional couplings are by far the minority. When a relationship is a means to an end, there is usually a perpetrator and a victim. One person is being used and manipulated. When one party intentionally veils or feigns their true intent in order to achieve a particular unstated end, that is simply nefarious behavior that victimizes the other party, regardless of how minimal or considerable the effect.

Why would someone treat another person like this? It all comes back to the end game we talked about in the last chapter. For these people, the end game is far more important than the feelings, time, and even the finances of the other person.

With that in mind, here are some reasons people pursue transactional relationships that are meant to be a means to an end.

1. **Esteem needs** – When people tie their self-esteem to their relationship status, or to their number of dating opportunities and choices, then who they are with becomes less important than the fact they are with someone. If the person you're with is simply there to be a stroke to your ego or a contribution to your cache, then they only serve a particular, defined purpose. Whether it is the trophy wife or the date that keeps you from showing up alone, it is all pride and ego. That ain't love.

2. **Sexual needs** – Sex is a human need, but biblically and morally it should be reserved for marriage. Everyone does not use the Bible as their standard for personal behavior, so in my communications, I like to cast a wider net and try to create content that is useful for all, Christians and non-Christians alike. With that said, too many relationships are driven by pursuit of sexual escapades and conquests, or because of the existence of sexual tension—or "chemistry"—between two people. There are those who live their lives vacillating between two dysfunctional extremes. At one extreme, they only pursue and engage with those they really want to have sex with. At the other, they satisfy their hormonal needs du jour with those who are willing to have sex with them at a given time. Among the myriad of problems with this

approach is, once the sexual excitement is gone, so is everything else.

3. **Financial assistance** – Let me say, from the outset, that the statements that follow are from my observations in urban, black America. I'm sure every other demographic has their stories as well. That said, I've seen single women consistently create financial obligations—i.e. children and all of the responsibilities of raising them. After getting their hearts broken several times, they seek out romantic companionship for the primary reason of enlisting someone to share in the financial burden. Please don't get me wrong. There are plenty of single women who work hard and take care of their children without the assistance of any man. I salute and applaud them. Nevertheless, the previously described women do exist. Unfortunately, desperate times can call for desperate measures. To be sure, using a financial liaison as a financial means to an end is in no way limited to females. Let's look at the other side of the coin as well. There seems to be an increasing number of men looking for a "sugar mama." They may soon even surpass the number of women looking for a "sugar daddy." Men who have reduced or eliminated their ability to be upwardly mobile or even employable often seek out women who will support them. It is actually quite pitiful to see, yet some who use women in this fashion choose to brag about it. I do not understand why.

4. **Obsession with the thought of being married** – Have you ever encountered someone who has become fixated on the idea of being married? I have, and it can

be a nerve-racking. From the constant first daters who try to find a perfect version of "the one," to women who are haunted by the supposed ticking of their biological clock, to men who just want to settle down with a good woman in hopes that will change the direction of their lives: they can all be a little annoying. They are engrossed with an image of their life as a husband or wife, and it dominates their thoughts. They see a picture in their mind, and they want it badly. Please understand, a desire to be married is healthy. A preoccupation with it can be very unhealthy. I've seen people marry and have children to check it off the list, accomplish the goal, or bring the picture in their minds to life. Like all relationship scenarios, it can end well, but there are those times it ends very badly. When it is time to be a wife or a husband and not just a bride or groom, the euphoria of achieving the goal tends to wane, and here comes real life with real marital responsibilities.

There are several other reasons people use relationships as a means to an end. They are too numerous to delineate in this short volume. Relationships of expediency usually do not end up at happily ever after. They can, but frequently they don't. There is a popular question in the business and personal development sectors: "What's your why?" I think it applies in relationships as well. Why you engage an individual romantically should be about the enjoyment, contentment, excitement, and fulfillment that your connection brings to each of you. Being together should be the only end game.

6

High End

Although my demographic was lower middle class for most of my childhood, it was important to my mother to expose us to some of the finer things in life. Most times, we really could not afford the experience that she had decided to give my siblings and me, but she did it anyway. She wanted us to at least be aware of what was available, and hopefully one day, possible. As a teen, my first fine dining restaurant experience was at Tony's in downtown St. Louis. I don't remember what I had to eat. I do remember that the servers were very attentive. I dropped my napkin, and my Super Server swooped down out of nowhere to pick it up and hand me a fresh one before I could reach down to retrieve it. The waitstaff also filled my water glass any time it was less than three quarters full. They came to the table so often it started to get on my nerves. I believe the first high-end department store she took us to was Saks Fifth Avenue, not Saks Off 5th, the outlet store, but the regular retail store. I looked at the prices and realized we had no business in there. My mom said that each of us could get one item. I chose a way overpriced designer sweatshirt.

I did not experience a luxury hotel until I was an adult.

The first time you stay in the Ritz Carlton, The Conrad, or a luxury boutique hotel will change your life. I must admit, I do not stay in them often, but I have a real affinity for luxury hotels. Initially, I was only a guest in these sorts of properties because I had been invited to speak and those were the accommodations chosen by my host. On one occasion, I looked at the room rate and thought to myself, "You better have your 'A' game when you speak tonight." Along with dining in fine restaurants and staying in fabulous hotels, I've worn high-end clothes and shoes, another affinity but those are purchases which my budget does not currently allow. Kudos go to my mom for teaching me how to dress well for less.

I remain grateful for the different points of my life where I have been blessed to experience some of the finer things in life. One thing I've learned from these experiences is that they all have one thing in common: the high-end items and experiences cost more. They are not always more satisfying, or of better quality or value, but they are always more expensive.

Relationships can have a high-end as well. For our purposes, the high-end of the relationship consists of the areas of the relationship that require you to do more and be better than what is normal or natural for you. Every romantic union places demands on the individuals participating in it. Some demands will be easier for you to satisfy than others. Earlier in the book, I wrote about the principle that each individual in the relationship has the responsibility to meet the needs and fulfill the expectations of his or her partner. The ability to effectuate your mate's satisfaction is in part tied to your own personal capacity. Pleasing your partner may require more or less from you, depending on what is normal or comes naturally for you. When it costs you more to satisfy and contribute to your mate, that is a high-end relationship area for you. The part of the relationship that requires your best effort to meet minimum standards, that, too, is a high-end area for you.

What is high-end for one person may not be for another. Factors include personality and emotional makeup, relationship experience and history, financial status, and even spirituality. People are different, which is why comparison can be a hindrance in relationships because it ignores individuality and personal variances. Often, we expect what is routine for us to also be routine for our mate. Have you ever been faced with this statement, "I don't understand why you can't just..."? How about this one? "That should just come naturally for someone you say you love." People are different, and their individuality determines what is and what is not natural, straightforward, or easy for them.

According the Myers-Briggs Type Indicator, my type indicator is INTJ. I am an introvert. I am more intuitive than I am sensing. I think more than I feel, and I use my judgement more than I use my perception. With my emotional composition, remaining open to being consistently interpersonally engaged and involved can be a high-end relationship requirement for me. Because of my personal makeup, at some point during the day, I have to be alone with no interpersonal demands placed on me. I am aware of my trait and how it can potentially negatively affect my relationship, so I have worked on it. I have learned to manage it much better. Because of my relationship history and experiences, I am very sensitive to angry conflict. When there is conflict and acrimony, they cause me to pay a larger emotional price than others potentially have to pay. Although conflict is a normal occurrence in any relationship, if it is not handled well, it gets very expensive for me. For me, it is a high-end area.

There is a cliché that says you get what you pay for. The service I received on occasion at The Ritz Carlton was worth the price of the room. I checked in at about 1am on a Sunday morning with an extremely wrinkled suit in my bag that needed to ready for me to wear 7 hours later and somehow my assistant forgot to pack dress socks. The hotel had dry cleaning facilities on property and a small clothing boutique. The bell captain told me to get some rest, and he would have both of my small emergencies handled by 7am. That level of service was worth the expense.

A great relationship makes paying the high-end price worth it as well. When it is the right person, being your best self or even increasing your personal capacity to meet relationship demands is a small sacrifice. When your partner pleases you in such a way that it adds significant value to your life and wellbeing, you willingly spend the necessary varied personal capital. It is not too high.

The key, though, is to recognize when you are getting what you're paying for. If the relationship is working, the other person is also putting in those high-end expenses to take care of you. Again, you get what you pay for. That goes for both partners in a relationship. If everyone is putting in their best and raising their capacity when necessary, both people will find their lives and relationships enriched.

7

Low End

Imagine being told by someone you were interested in that, before you could ever have a chance with them, there were some personal alterations you needed to make. I ask you to imagine it, but I don't have to. It happened to me once. To be completely transparent, I used the phrase personal alterations in order to satisfy my ego. To be more accurate, the person who put the demand on the table actually meant I needed to make some personal improvements. Think about the hubris, the unmitigated gall for such an insistence. She, in essence, told me I had to ameliorate myself in all the ways she envisioned to have a chance of initiating a romantic association her. Was she being lofty, too bold, and out of bounds? Or did she simply have some minimal standards for me to meet in order for the two of us to reach any conceivable potential?

It was the latter. To give even fuller disclosure, her demand was regarding my spirituality and the need to be more submissive and obedient to God. Who could argue against that? I certainly could not. Furthermore, as a principle, no one should be opposed to an individual having minimal personal standards for anyone who desires to enter into a romantic relationship with them.

So, let's talk about personal standards in amorous relationships. I was once asked for the best insight I had ever received regarding romantic alliances. It came from my friend, Michelle McKinney-Hammond. She told me that relationships are work. That advice was so good, it appears right at the beginning of this book. In my book, We Time, I also said, "Real love is work. It's a joy and a pleasure, but it is work."

Now, we all know that any job at a high performing organization will have both duties and minimum performance standards. According to a human resource document from Indiana University, performance standards "are the observable behaviors and actions which explain how the job is to be done, plus the results that are expected for satisfactory job performance. They tell the employee what a good job looks like." Minimum performance standards are the low end of what is required. It is what is expected from anyone who takes the position. I have never taken a job that I didn't believe I had what it took to be good enough to satisfactorily fulfill the duties of the job. In every job I've taken, I have known I possessed the talent, skill, and ability to at least be average. Hopefully, I could be stellar or even one of the best, but I knew I could handle the low end of the requirements. Otherwise, I wouldn't have taken the job.

Just as relationships have those high-end performance areas we already addressed, they also have low-end obligations. The low end is the minimum requirements in which you and your mate are confident you can perform. If the high end consists of the areas of the relationship that require you to do more and be better than what is normal or natural for you, the low end is the acceptable relationship conduct that should come naturally to you. Because it is innate or instinctive, low-end conduct is basic and should therefore be considered foundational. It should help provide the proper underpinnings on which to build your relationship dreams and establish the breadth of relationship potential. Potential begins with a determination of the baseline. What you believe is possible is usually grounded in some level of already verified truth. Even when the sky is the limit, or as Michael Jordan once famously said, "the ceiling is the roof," there is still a launching point. That's the low end. Low-end behavior is not sacrificial, exceptional, or outstanding. It is that which you can consistently expect to give and receive habitually, every day.

This brings us back to relationship foundations. We should all build our relationships based on what is available at ground level and not what we think we can reach in the heavens. Never decide to love your partner contingent upon his or her high-end behavior. It takes extra effort for your partner to reach that elevated end of your relationship. Since no one can constantly maintain extra effort, high-end comportment is usually intermittent and is not the proper material for a solid relationship foundation. Relationships should be based on the wonderful, habitual, basic behavior that two people offer each other. Not the extraordinary, but the ordinary. While I never want to be a minimalist, my ability to be exceptional is finite. If I create a situation where it takes the best of my ability to meet my wife's minimum standards, I am positioning myself for failure, and my wife is positioning herself for constant disappointment. I would rather my wonderful, habitual, basic behavior be satisfying to my discriminating partner. I would like for what comes naturally to me to set a high bar that I consistently meet and frequently raise.

Since the low end is the accepted and expected norm, failure to reach it should be considered an error, and habitual failure should be considered negligence. Your partner should be able to depend on low-end behavior always transpiring. As a rule, it should be invariable. It should be as unfailing as a good shake at Steak 'n Shake. Who has ever had a bad shake at Steak 'n Shake? I am sure it has happened, but not often. Whenever it happens, someone has certainly made a significant mistake. That's not to say there's no room for those mistakes. We all miss the mark from time to time. We can all have a bad day, but negligence has no place in your relationship. Neglect is a cancer. It can cause trust and even desire to erode. You have to habitually hold up the low end. You are obligated to routinely maintain the minimums. If you are invested in your relationship, that shouldn't be very hard.

However, while the constant handling of the low end should be expected and not too difficult to maintain, it should also be appreciated. There is a difference between being trusted and held accountable and being taken for granted. When a relationship is good, you should be thankful for the normal as well as the exceptional. When your partner consistently gives you the satisfaction you expect but also frequently gives you the amazing you do not expect, thank them for both. Additionally, when you know your mate has put in extra personal effort to please you in an area that doesn't come naturally to them, be extra grateful.

For the record, gratitude should be a low-end requirement in every relationship.

8

Making Ends Meet

Mississippi Masala is probably my least favorite Denzel Washington movie. Set in the Magnolia State, the 1991 film is a story of forbidden love between Washington's character, Demetrius, a carpet cleaner, and Mina, an Indian young lady whose family has fled the Ugandan dictator Idi Amin. Both of their families are against the relationship, but Demetrius and Mina eventually defy their families and run away together. This cinematic exposé on the survival of romance in a culture of racism and classism ends with Demetrius and Mina homeless, jobless, at odds with their families, but hugging and spinning in the middle of a field, happy to be in love and together.

After seeing this film, I remember walking out of the theater annoyed, especially at the ending. I was miffed that such a realistic drama would end in such an unrealistic way. Maybe my glass is half empty, but I felt like I knew what the rest of the story would be if Mississippi Masala was a real-life drama. There would have been a great deal of sadness and anguish in their future because of the incessant family and financial pressure. The odds against a black man and Indian woman in Mississippi in the 1970's, trying to build a life together without money, jobs, or high-paying skills, combined the lack of family support, would be almost insurmountable. Could they make it? Of course they could. Could the stress in their lives be so difficult that would cause their relationship to crumble? Of course it could. Would an eventual breakup be possible, even likely? Yes.

When ends do not meet, it is always a hardship on a relationship. Financial stress is one of the top causes of relationship failure. Romance and money are relatives, probably second cousins, but definitely bosom buddies. Money problems have an effect on everything else. It is difficult to be romantic, joyful, sensual, peaceful, or playful when bill collectors are constantly emailing and calling. Like the sight of blue lights behind you when a police officer is asking you to pull over, maneuvering around the lack basic necessities or being choked by a massive amount of debt can ruin your day. Unlike a speeding ticket, those money problems can ruin day after day. When the financial ends do not meet, the heart strings can become frayed. The hugging and the spinning are in jeopardy if the unit is not strong enough to withstand a storm of material and financial need.

There are some options that ensure money problems do not sabotage your relationship. If you are single, adequately prepare yourself prior to getting a mate and then make a good selection when you choose a partner. Through education, training, and/or entrepreneurship, secure the necessary earning potential to avoid the worst kinds of financial struggle. At the same time, increase your financial literacy and make sound financial decisions. If you are married, have a solid family financial plan and be sure to have enough margin in your household budget. Spend wisely and properly manage debt. If you are married and already in financial trouble, work out a plan now and execute it. Get help if you need it. Neutralizing the threat to your happiness and the future of your relationship should be a top priority.

I would like to say one more thing to those couples who are truly struggling to make basic ends meet. Remember you are teammates. Do not let the stress of the lack of basic necessities and the sacrifices and inconveniences they create cause you to turn on each other. I know that things like substandard housing, food, and clothing, along with a lower-than-desired quality of life for you and your children, can make you forget why you are in love, but fight to remember and remind each other. To the struggling middle class, do not allow the pressure of being overextended financially eat away at your union. Work through it, and by all means each of you hold up your end. It may not be 50-50 but do your part and play your role in the plan. Survive and then succeed as one. I love seeing the couples who struggled together get to enjoy a better life together. Their stories are uplifting. Each partner has their perspective on the history. They gladly tell their story and then they look at each other as if to say, "I'm glad we stuck it out."

9

Short End

I am a terrible negotiator. No, seriously I really am. I have three basic negotiation practices. 1. Refuse to negotiate. 2. Negotiate, but if it makes you angry, walk away. 3. Take the short end of the stick. The first reason I am a bad negotiator is I'm a little stubborn. If I have a strong belief or position on something I really care about, I may find it difficult to listen to another perspective or give ground. As I get older, and hopefully wiser and more mature, I have fewer personal non-negotiables, but where they exist, there really is no negotiating. Secondly, if the debate or contest of ideas and opinions concerns something or someone I love, the argument can start to feel personal, and then hypersensitivity can morph into anger. Since, as we've already discussed, I do not like unnecessary conflict or even necessary conflict in a touchy area, I may gracefully or not so gracefully bow out of the discussion to avoid any further emotional upheaval. At this point of my life, I would rather yield or feign understanding or agreement than fight with another individual.

I sometimes volunteer to take the short end of the stick for two reasons. If the negotiation is concerning something I do not really care about or do not have the time or interest to care about at the moment, then you win. I would rather not engage in the bargaining at all. You are right. I am wrong. You may do as you please. Can this just be over? The second reason is I do not like to feel as if I have taken advantage of anyone. I am good at argument; I am skilled at persuasion. Since I was a teenager, I have had some level of positional power. There were times in my younger years, I would win arguments and get my way because I could and not always because I was right. I have since been shown the errors of my ways and now have made drastic changes. Rather than wonder if I have unjustly wielded power or pushed a person into a corner to their own detriment, I would rather take the loss. This philosophy has caused me to be taken advantage of many times. I'm sure I don't always get the best possible price on purchases I make. I often yield to others when I should stick to my guns, and I am certain that most of my former employees were victorious in their salary and benefits negotiations. I learned to stay out of some human resource matters, so that the organization would not keep getting the short end.

That's not to say I like getting the shorter end of things. No one likes getting the short end of the stick, especially from their significant other. Let me say at the outset that just because you are not receiving what you desire or believe you deserve in your relationship, that does not automatically mean you are getting the short end. There are inequalities and imbalances that exist within every relationship that allow the individuals within the couple to complement and supplement each other. In other words, people possess different strengths and weaknesses. Relationships are not

50-50 at every point. You have a great relationship when two compatible individuals are viewed as equals and consistently give all they can to meet each other's needs and expectations without keeping score. You should not expect to receive back everything you give in equal quantities at all times. Of course, I am not speaking of areas such as fidelity, kindness, consideration, domestic involvement, etc., but people are different. Circumstances and situations will periodically change the relationship context, altering how partners are able to perform. A good thing to remember in all relationships is that people are not the same, and a change in circumstances can change how people function in the relationship, at least temporarily. Sameness in every area is not an attainable goal.

To make this a little more concrete, my wife cannot get equal time from me when it comes to preparing meals. I'm not built for it, and neither is my schedule. We have negotiated out a solution to this issue, and what we feel what we have decided is fair. Our agreement ensures she does not do all of the cooking all of the time. A professional athlete or coach may never have the amount of free time his or her spouse may require during the season. They have to agree on what is satisfactory for their relationship. Trying to split these things right down the middle won't just be frustrating for both parties, they'll be impossible. It's important to recognize that personal differences and an imbalance in performance in a particular sector of the relationship do not necessarily create a situation where an individual is getting the short end of the stick in the relationship. Poor choices and constant neglect do.

Your choice in a mate can set you up to receive the short end of the stick. If I have said that once, I have said it a thousand times, and at least a few times in this book. You are satisfied in a relationship when your partner fulfills your needs and meets your expectations. This only happens when the person you choose has the capacity and the willingness to do so.

That being true, why are we so eager to romantically connect with people who do not have what it takes to be who we need them to be? To be sure, there are those of you who ended up with the short end because they were hoodwinked into accepting the relationship equivalent of fool's gold. You dated an act for a while until to your dismay the real person appeared. How unfair it was for you to be bamboozled in such a way. Unfortunately, almost everybody has played the fool. You have my sympathy.

But sometimes, we volunteer to be disappointed. We allow other emotional and psychological factors or extenuating circumstances to cause us to stray from reason and gut feelings. We enlist ourselves in a relationship that is doomed to let us down because we chose a partner who we knew was lacking in ways which were unacceptable to us in the long term. We hope for a too significant of a change. People are who they are and not who we hope they will be. You can keep trying to make a nickel a quarter if you like, but you will be constantly short of change. A nickel can only be five cents. When you knowingly choose someone who is incapable of being the one, you should not complain about what you willingly created. Just correct it, if possible.

A second reason people find themselves with the short end of the stick is they have a partner who neglects them. Choosing a partner who does not have the capacity to be a proper mate for you is one thing. To have a significant other who has shown the ability to be what you need, but who is simply unwilling to do so on a regular basis, is something different all together. When someone is aware of your needs, is able to meet them, and chooses not to do so, then he or she has not made your longings a priority. When we consistently fail to show our mate that they are important, that is negligence. Negligence is corrosive to the long-term health of your relationship. It can cause significant deterioration, until one day, the neglected stops caring. They can become desensitized and detached, and eventually they can disappear. Why? Negligence breeds resentment.

As I've said above, all romantic relationships involve some level of risk. We all accept that. The deeper the commitment, the more the investment. Inherently, there is also some degree of spoken or unspoken bartering and bargaining between partners. Healthy relationships are those where no one is keeping score. In imbalanced, unhealthy relationships, the more you contribute, the more apt you become to evaluate what you receive. When someone gives their all and consistently gets the short end of the stick in return, they will develop resentment if their mate does not make the necessary alterations. If you want to protect your relationship from negligent behavior, be attentive to your partner and regularly show him or her that you care. Remember, relationships are work. Show up for work every day and clock in.

10

Book Ends

In our home, the dining room table seats eight people. There are three chairs on either side of an urban farmhouse table that my wife probably loves a little too much. For the two ends of her beloved table, she wanted chairs that made more of a statement than the others. While intently searching the internet for what seemed like days, she found what she was looking for, a wingback chair that was the proper seat height to fit under the table and that perfectly matched the other chairs that banked the sides of the table yet made the proper statement. There was one problem. The chair was very expensive, and we needed two of them. She chose not to immediately purchase them in hopes they would go on sale. They did not. With family coming to visit for the Christmas holiday, the wait for a price reduction ended. Time was up, and so, we ordered two expensive, regular priced wingback chairs that arrived in time for the holiday celebration. They look fantastic! One seat is hers; the other is mine. Like most families, we rarely have meals in the dining room, but when we do, it makes a great statement when we sit in our individual chairs. The man and woman of the house—co-leaders of the household—sit at the table as bookends for our children and any present guests. Although LuAnne and I usually prefer to sit next to each other during meals, we consciously or unconsciously make the statement during special occasions that there are two heads of our family.

Gender equality within romantic relationships is not as much of an issue as it used to be. Although there is still much work to be done, many Americans have evolved relative to the subject. There is only a remnant of people who continue to view women as second-class citizens, and people now embrace the fact that male headship is not synonymous with male superiority or domination. While some of the old guard still remain, the majority of people have chosen to be enlightened and to change their position and behavior. While boys and girls are different, I do not know any men who would say that their daughter is automatically personally inferior to a male by virtue of her gender. (I'm sure they exist. I just don't know any.)

With regard to romantic relationships, I find the verbiage we consistently use to describe people who engage in them to be revelatory. There is popular nomenclature to describe couples at every point in their relationship. For instance, I have performed numerous wedding ceremonies, and I always pronounce the man and woman "husband and wife." The pronouncement of the couple is never "husband along with his wife," or "I pronounce you husband, and secondarily I pronounce you his wife." There is no qualifier that says one is superior and another is inferior.

When two people are dating each other exclusively, we might call them "boyfriend and girlfriend." We also call unmarried, deep-end couples by universal terms such as "lovers" and "significant others." Earlier in the book, we discussed the fact that there are two ends to a relationship, and both parties have to hold up their end. In a sense, the two ends are bookends, metaphorically speaking. Literal bookends are support mechanisms that help keep a row of books upright. They are usually identical. They can be ornate or very simple, but together they do a job. If a relationship is to function at its optimal level, then, both partners will have to help it to be so. "It takes two to make a thing go right."

However, while bookends are usually identical, romantic partners never are. Instead, they should be compatible, so they can work together for the good of relationship. The best couples are united harmoniously. Harmony is perfectly blended individuality. When two individuals are compatible, they blend well together. They do not clash like musical notes improperly joined together. Discordant notes make a sound that clearly reveals they do not belong together. Incompatibility will always reveal itself as well. Unfortunately, it can take longer to recognize that two people do not mix than it takes to notice two notes do not blend. Compatibility is the proper mixture of similarities, commonalities, and differences. Two people can be tremendous individuals who should never attempt to be a couple because they are simply a bad match. They are too different to be able to work together to maintain a joint life together. They are not bookends. But, when two people have the right complimentary characteristics, view each other as equals, and choose to blend their individuality into a beautiful harmonious relationship that serves them well and keeps their joint life in its expected place, what wonderful bookends they make.

While a sense of equality and the existence of compatibility are necessary for couples to function together in a manner that leads to contentment, enjoyment, and fulfillment, there is one further ingredient that, when added to the relationship recipe, makes it a pièce de résistance. That additional element is purpose. Purpose is a reason for a relationship to exist that transcends the couple's contributions to each other. Purpose is the relationship's benefaction to the world in which it is contained. According to Genesis, when God created Adam and Eve, He gave their union purpose. God told Adam and Eve to be fruitful. He commanded them to use their union to be productive. The first romantic relationship in history was purpose-driven. They existed to do more than satisfy each other.

Bestselling author and marketing guru, Donald Miller, tells the story of crafting a business plan for his marriage, a "marriage plan," as he called it. With his wife's agreement, he decided that the mission for their marriage would be that they would have a restorative marriage. Their home would be a place of restoration. When he and his wife would come home from work, their purpose was to help restore each other, but also their home would be a place where others could come to be replenished. They intentionally have frequent guests and have built a home that sleeps 19, so that they can provide a place for people to be refreshed and rejuvenated. They not only work to please each other, but their life together has a purpose which they work together to fulfill.

Adam and Eve had a transcendent purpose. So does Donald Miller's marriage. Relationships that require work that goes beyond just meeting individual, parochial are strengthened by that purpose.

Equality, compatibility, and purpose make a great combination that can be used as rubric for evaluating new relationships. Whether or not the relationship satisfactorily answers the questions of equality, compatibility, and purpose is a great place to start when considering how deep you want a relationship to get.

I know some who are reading this are asking, "what about romance, chemistry, and eventually, love?" They, too, are important parts of the recipe for a relationship that has a happy ending. But you already knew to look for those qualities. Instead of seeking just love and chemistry, though, expand your palette and add some new ingredients. One collection of ingredients does not negate the other. You can have them all. You should.

11

Weekend

I know that it is a logistical impossibility for everyone to be off work on weekends, but I wish it was feasible. In my opinion, weekends should involve rest, recreation, worship, and occasionally, some community service. That is how you fill a weekend, or at least that is how I was conditioned as a child. Friday evenings, Saturdays, and Sundays were the best times as a kid. Each week, we filled those two days like they were five, with sports, recreation, entertainment, and church. There were no video games in those days. The streets were safer, and I would like to think we were less mischievous than children today. But maybe we weren't.

As an adult, I became consumed with my career goals and ministry responsibilities. I was driven to be successful. For much too long, I ignored how important it is for couples to make time for relaxation and recreation. My life was completely out of balance. I always made time for recreation with my children but did not realize how important it was to do the same with my spouse. I wish I had. I wasted so much precious time and squandered opportunities and possibilities. Couples need time to relax and have fun together. Life is always demanding and frequently difficult.

Everyone gets stressed, but it is important to avoiding getting stressed out. When individuals are stressed out, they often turn on their partner rather than turning to them. Healthy ways of relieving stress are paramount, and couples should take some "we time" and have fun together.

Years ago, I learned that, if you have a job that demands a great deal from you mentally, just getting rest will not completely rejuvenate you. People who work hard also need to play hard. Playing hard as a couple, though, means a mix of compromise and finding what you both love doing.

A year of my weekends will include a mix of activities for me, for my wife, and for both of us. My wife rarely likes to sit around the house on weekends. Usually, around Wednesday, weekend activities are discussed. Sometimes, those plans are mostly for her. My wife loves the beach or sitting all day on a nice pool deck. It is not my favorite thing in the world, but I like to enjoy the things she takes pleasure in with her. Other weekends, we'll do something that's more for me. We are both sports fans, but I am a sports fanatic, in the literal since. I love watching sports on television but attending live sporting events has become my thing. We attend them together. We live in central Florida. Recently, we drove to Tampa to watch my baseball team, the New York Yankees, lose a spring training game to my childhood team, the St. Louis Cardinals. Afterwards, we drove another two hours to Gainesville to watch my basketball team, the Florida Gators, lose to LSU in overtime. We then made the two-hour drive home, arriving just before midnight. I took two losses that day, but spending that down time with each other was a win for our relationship.

Vacations are great for some concentrated couple time that allows for both people to have their favorite types of relaxation and fun. We take an international one biennially. On those trips, we get to explore new cultures and food while relaxing and making some great memories. I love those vacations, but vacations are no excuse to ignore those less ambitious, less adventurous weekend activities. By all means, travel the world, but do not forget about just doing fun, inexpensive things on a consistent basis as well. It helps build an even stronger bond.

12

YEAR-END

When I was a pastor, I had mixed feelings about year-end meetings. I believe in the importance of the assessment and evaluation of the organization, but my staff of employees and volunteers will tell you I was not quite fond of employee and volunteer performance evaluations. The failure to give adequate feedback to my workers was one of my weaknesses as a leader and manager. I learned to leave the human resource concerns to the church administrator. On the other hand, with the exception of the financial reports—I can only focus on numbers for about 45 minutes before I check out—I liked looking at the year-end data that told the story of how the organization had performed. The data helped me to be objective in my assessment of what we were doing, and the information helped me plan for the future. It was important to set goals for the following year that were at the very least grounded in the truth of the previous year's performance.

Do you and your partner have a year-end meeting about your relationship? Is there any year-end reporting of partner performance and relationship contentment, fulfillment, and enjoyment? At the beginning of the year, many couples make plans, set goals, and hopefully remind each other of their individual dominant needs and expectations. But what good are plans, goal setting, and information exchange at the beginning of the year if there is no assessment at the end of it? Some would say that intentionally evaluating your relationship is asking for trouble. Leave well enough alone. If it ain't broke, don't fix it. Don't rock the boat. I disagree with this sentiment. We constantly evaluate what's going on in our relationship, consciously or unconsciously. We draw conclusions, make decisions and make adjustments based on our own, unspoken assessments. Since facts and opinions evoke emotions, we start to feel a certain way about our relationship, good or bad or both. At the same time, our partner does not know what is going on until a situation reveals what his or her mate has been thinking and feeling for some time.

People die of treatable illnesses because they refuse to seek medical evaluation, care, and treatment. Relationships can be damaged and die from an explosion caused by some complaint that has been building for years or from long-term neglect, all because both partners chose not to communicate their personal thoughts and feelings to each other in a timely and systematic manner. Remember, the objective of your relation is not to "leave well enough alone," it's to have the best relationship possible. In organizational behavior, there is a saying that whatever is measured improves and whatever is measured and reported improves faster. I do not know about you, but I want to know if I am doing well as partner. I may think I am, but I need to hear it from my wife. I want to know if she is satisfied with me as a husband. I would like it to be verified that we are reaching any relationship goals and objectives we might set. I desire to be aware of any areas I need to improve. I do not want to lose my wife's smile over something that could have been fixed. For that reason, I ask her how I am doing on a regular basis.

I also ask her how she is doing and if there is any new information about her of which I should be made aware. Here is why. People change; their likes and dislikes, tastes, viewpoints, and even their wants and needs change. Just like with your computer or smart phone, it is important to get updates from your mate and download them. If we are not aware of the changes in our significant other, we will continue to relate to who they once were. For example, I know most of my wife's favorites. For example, I know her favorite foods, her favorite way to relax, her favorite coffee, and her favorite dress designers. I would like to say I know them all of her favorites, but I will leave some margin for potential error or ignorance. If her favorites change, and I am not aware, then she will not receive from me what she really desires. Furthermore, I would be deluded because I would have concluded I hit the target dead center, when in reality, I missed the mark. For that reason, I check for updates. I want her to be happy in our relationship. I want her to keep smiling. I want our story to have a happy ending.

13

Loose Ends

"I like you. I'm interested. As a matter of fact, I've often tried to imagine what it would be like to date you—I mean all out pursue you—but now is just not a good time." Those are the words of a wise, thoughtful man who had taken inventory of his life and knew what he should and should not do. Wesley was a divorced father of a 9-year-old son. He met Karen at the gym. They would see each other from time to time, and one day, they struck a conversation after their workouts. They exchanged numbers and email addresses and agreed to meet for coffee. Meeting for coffee became a periodic habit that went on for a couple of months. They had great conversations and seem to enjoy each other's company. As time went on, Karen could not figure out why Wesley had not asked her out on a real date, so she asked him a question. "Do you ever want to do anything else, like catch dinner of something?" Wesley gave his thoughtful response that conveyed his romantic attraction, but told her, "now is just not a good time."

If the attraction was there, why was it not a good time? Wesley had some loose ends he needed to tie up before he could consider seriously dating Karen. There were some things he needed to settle before adding another relationship variable to his life's equation. He was in a child support and visitation dispute with his ex-wife that could potentially evolve into a child custody battle. He was current on his payments, and whatever else his son needed, he tried to make it happen. He loved his son, was very active in his life, and was trying his best to shield his son from the effects of the animosity that existed between him and his ex-wife. The volatility of the situation left his life extremely unsettled. At that moment, there was no room for Karen in his life. He wanted to tie up loose ends before entering what he thought could become a deep-end relationship.

We all have unfinished business from time to time. Wesley was 38 years old, and the older you are, the less likely that you will come to a new relationship tabula rasa, with a clean slate. Periodically, we have things we dealing with, life stuff that takes our time, mental and emotional energy, and even our financial resources. Sometimes, we cannot and should not move forward in our romantic relationship life until we have satisfactorily settled those issues. Relationships can get off to a bad start because they are initiated in a mine field. When you are presently engaged in situations such as active drama from a past relationship, severe financial issues, a health crises with a loved one, the pursuit of a graduate degree, or the launching a business, it may not be a good time to start a new relationship or move a present one to the next level.

Life is never perfect and rarely without difficulty or challenge. But some circumstances can create too much instability and irregularity. They require the lion's share of your time and energy. They do not leave room for any increase in your relationship responsibilities. When there are loose ends that have the potential to affect the present and the future, it is best to tie them up before adding new strands of interpersonal complexity that can tie you knots. Your life should have a functioning amount of cohesion before adding new or increased obligations in the area of romance. We have to be wise and disciplined enough not to over-commit ourselves, regardless of the opportunity and our interest in it. Sometimes, you have to stand pat. In the words of Kenny Rogers, "You've got to know when to hold 'em, know when to fold 'em, know when to walk away, and know when to run."

Wesley taught Karen a very important lesson: everyone who is single is not available. There is a corresponding lesson for those who are already in a relationship, especially if it has reached the deep end. A person can desire to marry you but know it is not the right time.

Karen had a choice to make. She could respect Wesley's position, or she could try to force the issue, since she knew he was interested. If she chose to respect his position, she would have to wait for this desired romance to actually begin. If she gave him reasons why waiting was unnecessary—she's a big girl; she can handle whatever is going on in his life; putting things on pause reduces how much support she can give him during this difficult time—she could potentially convince him to move ahead with a dating relationship with her. The question would then be: at what cost? Things might go fine, or they might become more complicated and stressful than they otherwise would have. Relationships take time, energy, and focus, all of which can be sparse when you are engaged in tying up major loose ends. The safest bet for Karen would be to give Wesley the time that he needed to shore up things in his personal life, especially since it involved his son.

Karen was wise. She did not try to force the issue. But she did have a question that she needed answered.

"Are you over your ex?" she asked. Wesley responded, "Yes, completely. My only desire is that we be able to effectively co-parent." Karen inquired about a most important potential loose end, when the ex- is not fully an ex-. A new relationship should not begin until the previous one has truly ended. It is difficult to build toward the future when the past is lingering or loitering in the present. Some people attempt to assuage the pain of a breakup with a new hookup. Usually, it does not work. We either stunt the real progress of the present relationship or kill it altogether because we are emotionally torn. Even when our attention and affection are limited to our present commitment, we can still be attached to our past connection. I cannot stress how important it is to tie up the loose ends of a former relationship. Karen knew the importance and wanted to be sure.

One final thought. Loose ends do not tie themselves. When we face ongoing, unsettling situations, often there is a tendency to abdicate our responsibility to take action. There are times when saying, "I'm praying about it. It is in God's hands" or, "It will work itself out" is a copout and a dereliction of duty. We have to be willing to personally take action to address the things that can hinder our future.

To tie up loose ends, we may have to engage in difficult conversations, make tough choices, or be brutally honest with ourselves and act accordingly. Whether you need to address a financial or legal situation, settle things legally or emotionally with your ex-, or seek help to fix something that is broken in you, to the best of your ability, do the work to bring those things that are unnecessarily lingering to a conclusion. Create some margin in your life. Clear up some space, so you can have room for what you want to do next.

14

Split Ends

Journey with me back to the early 1980's in the black community. Let's take a look into salons, kitchens, basements, front and back porches. All places where females young and old would get their hair done. This was prior to box braids, weaves, extensions, lace fronts, and today's popular wigs. In the 80's, females were getting their natural hair braided, pressed with a hot comb, and permed. As an outside male looking in, it seemed as if they were all looking to grow their hair to be as long as possible. The sassy short styles of present day were not in vogue at the time. For teens and young adult ladies, length was king, or should I say, queen.

"You have split ends" was an announcement that ladies did not like to hear. It meant that the cuticles of their hair had been worn down, and the ends had become frayed, damaged. Getting split ends periodically is basically unavoidable. They cannot be cured; they must be clipped. If not, the damage continues upward toward the root, losing length but, more importantly, making hair less healthy. Early detection and elimination help to mitigate the harm done to the hair follicles. Clip, clip, and the problem is solved.

Developing split ends is normal. Developing split ends in your relationship is also normal, but you have to do everything in your power to clip, clip the troubled spots and repair them as quickly as possible and at all cost. It is a fact that no one is error free. You can be loving, faithful and keep all of the other vows you made at the altar or the courthouse, yet you will make mistakes, bad decisions, and have lapses in judgement. You may be absent when you needed to be present. You might do the wrong thing with the right motives. On occasion, your words may not come out just right. It will happen. You may frustrate or disappoint your partner or cause them pain. Those things do not necessarily cause damage. Damage is different from hurt or mere pain. Where there is damage, there is injury. Something has been broken or shattered. Some damage happens in an instant, like setting your hair on fire. Other types develop more slowly, and as with split ends, early detection and treatment are critical if you want to avoid more significant harm.

You make two primary contributions to your relationship, your words and your actions. Words are extremely powerful. In the Bible, Proverbs 18:21 says, "The tongue has the power of life and death." No doubt your relationship began in part because of great conversation filled with affirming and complimentary language. During the same relationship, unfortunately, words can also be used as a weapon and become potential causes of damage to your partner or to your union. As children, we were incorrectly taught that sticks and stones break bones, but words cannot hurt us. We have all discovered that words can hurt, and they can do damage. Words matter. Words can ruin another person's self-perception. They can be used to manipulate emotions and color reality. You can injure or kill your relationship with bad communication habits and patterns. Here is a list of what I call "shotgun statements." These statements have immediate and a potentially long-term effect on your relationship, no matter how you say them. If you say them, whether you mean them or not, know that you have fired a shot, and most likely, you have done some damage.

1. My family (or a particular family member) doesn't like you.
2. I don't like your family (or a particular family member).
3. I cannot believe I ever hooked up with you in the first place
4. You were just something to do.

I am sure you can add to the list. These shotgun statements are further proof the cliché about words never hurting is not true.

There is another adage I have found does have some veracity. I am sure you have heard this one. "It's not what you say, it's how you say it." Since I happen to be a natural smart aleck and can unknowingly have a sharp tongue at times, I have heard this one countless times. The way you say something can indeed be as important as the verbiage used. Tone and volume matter when speaking. It is important to monitor them both, especially when you are angry. Do not let your emotions have undue power over what you say and how you speak to your significant other. Stay in control, even when hurt or angry. Everyone has a different sensitivity to aggressive or angry communication, and we all like to be spoken to in a certain manner, regardless of the situation.

Be aware of your own sensitivity and your partner's. Have a discussion and make some determinations and commitments about how you will speak to each other and comply with them. Relationships involve many different covenants. An agreement on how you will communicate with each other most certainly should be one of them. This can help you avoid unnecessary damage.

A third aphorism is relevant to the discussion. I am sure you have heard this one. "Actions speak louder than words." Your actions are your second fundamental input to your relationship. A thousand words cannot create one action, but one action can justify or eliminate a thousand words. Make sure your words and actions are congruent with each other. Do what you say. Do not overpromise and underperform. Promises that are made but not kept can cause disappointment, destroy trust, and build resentment. In the words of my friend, Hart Ramsey, "Repeated disappointment can permanently cripple a once hopeful heart." Severe damage is done when your mate becomes conditioned to ignore your words because of the track record of your performance.

I hope by now someone is asking, "What do you do when the damage is already done?" I have good news for you. Like the damage split ends do to your hair, damage to your relationship can be repaired, and for the sake of the future of your relationship, it must be. Hurt and pain can dissipate over time, but where there is damage, there is impairment. Anything that is impaired is not in its prescribed condition and cannot function optimally. Damage has to be repaired for the good of the relationship. When it is not addressed, deterioration can take place. And just like a split end working its way to the root, the longer you wait the more you potentially lose.

Repairing the harm done to your relationship or your partner starts with accepting that it exists and dealing with its cause. If you do not face it, you cannot fix it. You and your mate should have honest conversations, address the source of the damage, and develop a plan to fix it and avoid it in the future. If you need help from a counselor or therapist, get it. Your relationship is worth it. Please remember, an accident can wreck a car in a second. It may take months to repair it. Fixing your relationship may take time. Be patient.

15

End Around

Once, I watched an ESPN documentary about high school football players from the small, south Florida region they call Muck City. The area is located in the Florida Everglades, on the banks of Lake Okeechobee. Muck City has two towns, Pahokee and Belle Glades. This rural area has produced over 60 NFL players since 1980, and it is known for speedy running backs, receivers, and defensive backs. While watching the documentary, I could not believe what I was seeing. High school coaches had converged on an open field to watch young men chase rabbits. They rated the speed of young football players based on how quickly they could catch a rabbit. One coach who was interviewed said he used this exercise to decide what position the adolescent players would play. This was an unorthodox way for a coach to assess and position players. They were not being timed in the 40-yard dash on a track. They were not doing cone drills on a football field. They were being clocked as they chased rabbits.

Football coaches love having speed on the edge. There is a popular saying among football coaches: "You can't teach speed." An offense with elite speed will invariably run a play called the "end around." This misdirection play is effective when you have a speedy player on the edge. For spectators, it is fun to watch. The end starts on one side of the line of scrimmage, takes the ball, and runs around the edge of the opposite side avoiding most of the defensive line. If he gets blocks on the edge, the play usually gets big yardage. It is even a quick way for a team to score a touchdown. I used to love watching the speedy Percy Harvin, when he was a Florida Gator, or the lightning fast Devin Hester, when he was a Miami Hurricane, run this play. It was an offensive weapon for both teams.

However, while using the end around to avoid the defense is effective in the sport of football, it is usually a totally ineffective relationship strategy when dealing with conflict. I would not advise you to have it in your playbook.

There are two basic areas of avoidance in a relationship: intimacy and conflict. Exploring the causes and effects of the former are outside the scope of my ability, so I will focus on the latter. Before we get to that, though, let me first admit that the metaphor above is not exact. In football the defense is the opposition. In relationships, your partner should never be viewed as your opponent. When there is a conflict, the goal is not defeating your partner and winning. You and your partner may be on opposite sides of an issue, but you are on the same team. You are not opponents; you are partners living life together through the good and the bad. Your objective is not to score. Resolution is the goal. You simply want to solve a problem or find a compromise, so you can protect or reestablish the peace and harmony in your union. In the Bible, Jesus says that blessed are the peacemakers. I was once taught peace does not always come on its own. Frequently, it has to be made. In other words, you have to face problems in order to fix them. They are not always avoidable. For the health of the relationship, we shouldn't try to run an end around on our problems, we should address them.

Avoidance is dangerous to the health of the relationship—and potentially jeopardizes its future—because it is a sign of weakness in the relationship. Most likely, it is also a sign that the person who employs it is either fragile, secretive, or indifferent. When a relationship is strong, there is no need to run from disagreement, disappointment, or trouble. In a good partnership built on a solid foundation, there is enough security for the individuals within the couple to face a challenge together head on. A couple is able to use its joint strength, complementary skills and abilities, and commitment to each other to overcome a setback, conquer any situation, or span any divide. There is no need to evade, pretend, hide, or ignore.

Let's break down those three character flaws that lead to avoidance, starting with emotionally fragility. Some people only pretend that everything is always all right. It is easier that way. They are so sensitive that any type of negativity or tension sends them reeling. In their minds, all problems are potentially big problems, so it is important that there are no problems at all. If they lack confidence in their mate's love, support, and commitment to them, any sign of unhappiness, disenchantment, or disagreement is viewed as having the potential to end the relationship. Fragile people will frequently run the end around, and it is not healthy for them or the relationship in the long run. Sooner or later, they will crack because pretense siphons one's strength and does not cultivate real joy. Masquerading and pretending to be happy is very tiring.

With secrecy, you avoid the subject, situation and your significant other because you have something to hide. Those with something to hide can use several types of avoidance techniques. They may continually punt on disagreements, trying to delay the confrontation. They say, "Let's talk about it another time." The right time never comes. Emotional meltdowns are also a useful tactic. They can lose their temper during the encounter, become irascible, and make it impossible to continue the discussion. Another method is to express hurt feelings that potentially make one's partner so sympathetic that he or she drops the issue altogether. This is a dastardly act if the confronted individual is actually feigning the hurt feelings in order to hide something from their partner.

A final reason for avoidance is personal indifference. I wish you could feel my apprehension as I write this paragraph. I am bothered by the mere thought of indifference existing in a romantic union. Everything changes when somebody stops caring. When a partner truly becomes apathetic about the relationship, true intimacy is hindered or even eliminated, and the couple's days are probably numbered. When an individual has stopped caring, they avoid confrontation because it is simply not worth the trouble. He or she has emotionally flatlined. There are no real peaks and valleys. If things are good, fine. If things are bad, fine. He or she does not care anymore. When people get to this point, they avoid confrontation so as not to disturb the dysfunctional version of peace they have manufactured. They have reached a resolve. They think, and in some cases, articulate a word that sums up their apathy. That word is "whatever." When avoidance is birthed from indifference, this end around may lose the game for you.

No matter the reason, though, if you are running the end around on your partner, you have to stop. Avoidance doesn't make problems in a relationship disappear. Unlike a football game, there's no clock counting down to when you go home. A problem will remain a problem until you address it. If the problem is indifference, a secret, or a deep sensitivity or insecurity, now is the time to address that, too. Facing a problem or a conflict is what your relationship is built to do. If you've gotten the other elements right, it will be able to handle whatever difficulties you have ahead.

16

At Wit's End

"I quit." "I'm out." "Just leave." "I can't do this anymore." "I think we should go our separate ways." "Don't call me ever again." "I just signed my divorce papers." "We just grew apart." "It just didn't work out." "Do what you have to do." "This is just not working." "I don't want to do this anymore." "I'm done." "It's over." "I just couldn't make it work."

I am sure you are familiar with one or more of these statements. They are all associated with a relationship that is ending or has ended. They're the words of a breakup. Since the average relationship lasts two years and nine months, there is now a tremendous amount of research that has been done on why couples break up. I have viewed numerous lists chronicling the top reasons relationships fail. The lists are different, but these seem to make every list in some form:

1. Trust issues
2. Money problems
3. Narcissism and selfishness
4. Not enough sex
5. Infidelity

6. Communication Issues
7. Incompatibility

Conspicuously absent from all these lists is what I believe is perhaps the most common reason for relationship failure: the lack of coping and problem-solving skills among the individuals within romantic relationships. In many cases, people are ill-equipped to effectively address relationship difficulty. They do not know what to do when the relationship falls on really hard times. When exhilaration turns into exasperation and the Little House on the Prairie becomes the Nightmare on Elm Street, people without the proper relationship and interpersonal skills are at a loss. They don't know how to get things back to where they need to be. The options become fight or flight. The poisonous cocktail of hurt, anger, fatigue, frustration, and desperation is daily administered intravenously to the individuals within the couple. It flows through their veins because when there are severe relationship issues, the situation affects your total being and almost everything you do. People who care deeply, even love each other, reach their wit's end and someone finally says, "I can't do this anymore." The relationship ends, and in many cases, unnecessarily.

I have tried to pick up the game of golf on several occasions. The game can be deeply frustrating for me. The body movements are so unnatural. Once, I was on the driving range, having very little success hitting the ball straight or with any distance to speak of. A couple of times, I hit a good shot. Oh the joy! The next 15 were terrible, but that one straight shot gave me the motivation to continue. I kept hitting ball after ball with no improvement to my average.

I got so annoyed. I was failing, and it was not due to the lack of effort. I was trying, I knew I was doing something wrong, but I did not know what. I kept trying. It was futile. I did not have enough golf knowledge or skill to diagnose my problem or do anything about it. When you don't know, you don't know.

For me, golf involved being terrible at something that I was investing time, energy, and resources in. I was trying to enjoy something I was not good it. When it went well, I did not know why. When it went wrong, I did not know how to fix it. Unfortunately, this is the plight of so many when it comes to romantic relationships. We want to succeed in our romantic alliances but do not have the knowledge and skills to be good at them. When things go wrong, we are not equipped with the power to functionally cope. We do not have the requisite ability to problem solve. We get frustrated, tired, and desperate. We reach our wit's end. Sometimes, you are ready to face it, but you do not know how to fix it. In that case, what should we do? We should get some help, the right help.

Before I address the importance of getting assistance during significant relationship trouble, though, I must address one other issue. It is important to create enough mental and psychological margin for pain and disappointment. False expectations of perfection or something close to it create a relationship where there is no room left for injury, difficulty, or agony. Sustained relationship problems become too much of a shock to our systems, an unexpected slap in the face and a punch in stomach. To be clear, as you know by now, I am not a proponent of setting low expectations or having none just so you can avoid disappointment. I think, when two people make good partner selections and commit wholeheartedly to their union, they should have the highest of hopes. Nevertheless, to eliminate the potential for trouble and tears from your calculations concerning your future with your significant other is presumptuous, unwise, and a little immature. We've already explored how the person who loves you can disappoint you, even when they're doing everything right. If you are going to actively love someone for a long time, you will eventually have to forgive them of something. I am not saying you should operate your relationship without principles, boundaries, or standards, but please create margin for your relationship to recover from mishap and difficulty. And, when necessary, get some help. The future of your relationship may depend on it.

You may be doing all you know and all you can, but all that you know is not all that there is to know, and someone else may be able to do what you cannot. Why should you limit your options to your knowledge, skill, perceptions, and abilities alone? That frustrating day on the golf range, I made a decision. My only hope of improving was to get some help. I needed a coach, someone whose knowledge far exceeded mine. Otherwise, I would keep trying and failing. We do not draw a similar conclusion often enough when it comes to our relationships. Could it be that when I reach my wits end that I need to enlist and incorporate someone else's wit? Many relationships end prematurely and avoidably because we do not seek out the proper assistance.

We ventilate to people we trust. We all need someone to talk to about what we may be experiencing, especially when we are in despair. Emotional support and a listening ear are so helpful, yet not all who support should advise. If we are not careful, we can take advice from someone who should be limited to encouragement, prayer, a listening ear, and a hug. They are not qualified to give advice. They may not have the knowledge, ability, or objectivity to help you, and the wrong help can make things worse or interfere with your ability to get better.

So, get the right help. Seek out a competent pastor. Search for the relationship counselor or licensed therapist that is right for you. It may take a little trial and error, and I know that can be difficult when you are already in pain and emotionally fatigued. Push through. If we have a physical condition, and we have to research and consult to find the right doctor, we do it. We do not decide to just live with it or die from it. We do what's necessary to find a cure. Or we should. Just as too many people die from preventable or treatable diseases, too many relationships succumb, even though an antidote to their problems exists, if they would only seek some expert help. Relationship trauma can be a heavy load. There are those trained to help you carry the load properly and teach you how to get rid of it. Let them help you.

17

Dead End

When I was a teen, we lived in a house located on a dead-end street for a couple of years. I have several bad memories from our time at that house. The fact that the house was on a dead-end street was appropriate. Many things came to a halt or were lost, broken, or stolen during our time there, including my 24-inch yellow Schwinn ten speed bike with the yellow seat with the tar stain on it from when I had fallen coming down "suicide hill" in my hometown of East St. Louis, Illinois. Can you tell I am still miffed about my bike?

For all that, the neighborhood was decent. There were plenty of other kids, and we played a lot of basketball. The street was our court. At first, the rim and the plywood used for a backboard were nailed to a tree in front of our house. My mother did not like that. That area got too crowded, and there was too much traffic because our house was near an intersection. Someone in the neighborhood decided to move our basketball court to a wooden telephone pole at the dead end of the street. There were no homes down there, so we would not be disturbing any one, and no one would disturb us. "Let's go down to the dead end" became the normal cry of the boys on our street. It meant we were going to play basketball. The dead end of the street served our purpose. It was where we played. It was where the girls crowded around to watched us play. It was our spot.

No one says, “Let’s go down to the dead end” when they are starting a relationship, but many people end up there all the same because they initiate relationships that are headed toward a dead-end from the start. Dead-end relationships are those that do not have the ingredients necessary to be long-term. They are short-term with limited potential because they are inherently flawed. Dead-end relationships are not a calculated risk. They are not a matter of hit or miss. They are a definite strikeout just waiting to happen. The only mystery is how long the at-bat will last. When dead-end relationships are born, death is imminent. They do not blossom or flourish for long. They do not have what it takes to last.

There are two general types of dead-end relationships: the “anyway” and the affair. The “anyway” relationship is the type where people knowingly and voluntarily select a partner to whom they are not a proper match, or they willingly enter a relationship fully aware that it is not the proper time. They did it anyway. The “anyway” relationship is a conscious decision to enter a subpar situation they know cannot last. There is too much incapability. There is a verifiable lack of capacity. The age gap is too wide. A person is emotionally unavailable. An individual is on the rebound. A suitor is still in love with his or her ex-. One or more of these and other red flags are there, but we choose to start the relationship anyway. Have you heard people’s postgame statements, once they reached the inevitable dead end? "I was having fun. I did not care if it wasn't going to last." "I had my reservations from the beginning, but I thought I would give it shot." They were not fooled. They did not make a mistake. They were not victimized. They knew better but did it anyway.

The willingness to enter an "anyway" relationship (as well as an affair, as we will discuss next) is rooted in a need for instant gratification. Despite the fact that the relationship will end at a dead-end, it serves a purpose right now. It meets an immediate need. As we already know, esteem, connection, and sexual needs scream loudly to be met, and these relationships can temporarily fulfill those needs. These needs don't care about sound reasoning or long-term potential. Esteem, connection, and sexual needs just want to be satisfied now. We can have every reason to evade a particular relationship encounter, but we will move forward with it anyway to satisfy an intense need. The key to overcoming the "anyway" tendency is discipline, and discipline presupposes a dimension of self-denial. Your ability to change your choice from "anyway" to "no way" will be contingent upon your capacity for self-denial and how much you truly value your time, energy, resources, and in some cases, how meaningful sex needs to be to you.

The second type of dead-end relationship is the affair, and just like the "anyway" relationship, it is a selfish act. Forbidden love affairs have been a part of human history since ancient times. A few are even chronicled in the Bible. Since humans began to populate the earth, men and women have been engaging in proscribed romantic relationships. In every era, on every continent, among all religions, races, and ethnicities, it happens. Men and women cross lines and have verboten romantic liaisons. Regardless of the context or backstory, the overwhelming majority of them have a couple things in common: they don't end well, and they cause damage.

Why do dead-end forbidden relationships happen so frequently? Is it because we are all inherently sinful? Is it because we can be selfish, shallow, and short-sighted, shielding our eyes from looking at the danger down the road? Are our immediate needs or long-suppressed desires so powerful that we choose to enjoy the ride even though it is on a dangerous street that draws to a close at a dead end? Do we not care about the wasted time? How do we become so desensitized to the potential hurt and pain we will cause someone else? The answers to all of these questions come back to the issues we've already covered in this book. If you aren't beginning relationships well, and keeping relationships healthy, you create more scenarios where you may enter an "anyway" relationship or enter an affair.

We should try to learn the dangers of dead ends upfront, so we don't allow ourselves to go down those roads when they present themselves. Since dead ends have no exits, once you reach them, there are only two choices: buy or rent so you can stick around down there or turn and go back the way you came. Whatever the choice, you'll find yourself the lesser for it. There will be collateral damage. Something will be lost.

18

The End

(An Open Letter)

Relationships end. Either by death or decision, people part ways. Since I am ill-equipped to address the myriad of issues that accompany the death of a partner in love, I have chosen to only focus on the latter. For those of you who lost your loving partner in death, you have my prayers and my sincere condolences. I pray that time will heal you and that God will give you the strength to renew your life as you move forward. Please avail yourself to grief counseling, if necessary.

Here, though, let's concentrate on relationships that end because of a decision. When people decide to end their relationship, we often call it a breakup. If you made that decision, I trust it was the right one and that you have no regrets in the future. Hopefully, you called it off in an honorable way, and there was no drama and the least amount of acrimony possible. If the decision was mutual, I wish you both well as you recover, regroup, and move forward with your lives. If there are children under 21 involved, please compartmentalize your role as parents and meet the needs of your children, despite any negative feelings you may have for your ex-. The children need the healthiest situation possible. It is important to soften the blow for them. If there are adult children, communication is key. Each child will react and respond differently and have his or her own individual needs. Be a good parent, even when you are in pain.

For those who did not make the decision to end their relationship, breakups are the most difficult. You are my primary focus at this time. To know what to do next, you first have to determine if your relationship is really over. If you want it to be, then fine. Some people know their relationship should end but for their own reasons will not act on their true desire. They leave it to their partner to initiate parting of ways. That can be an act of cowardice, but the result is the same. If you did not want the breakup and believe that it was premature, the question that is on the table now is: are you willing to fight for a reconciliation? I dare not advise you on whether or not you should fight or how long. Romantic relationship restoration and reunification are complicated subjects to broach, especially for people of faith. There are no exact answers. Many relationships have been restored because someone refused to give up and kept believing God would affect a reconciliation. On the other hand, many people have stunted their lives because they could not discern the difference between giving up and letting go. Just be prayerful and wise.

If the relationship is truly over, it will be important that you accept it. It is not healthy to constantly live in denial, though denial is often used as anesthesia for the pain. The pain of a breakup is real. It can be devastating. Breakups have caused many emotional breakdowns. The pain can be intense and even overwhelming. I encourage you to manage it. You cannot ignore it, and you cannot make it hurry up and go away. You cannot even pray it away. I know. The pain is real and intense. Please do not use chemical substances, a rebound relationship, your job or business, or your children to try to avoid it. Try to effectively regulate yourself while feeling it. Pain can cause people to do things they would not normally do. With time, the support of loved ones, and therapy (if necessary), you will heal and recover. Know the healing process cannot begin until you have accepted that the relationship is over.

After accepting the new reality, take responsibility for any contribution you made for the relationship ending. Just because you did not make the decision to call it all off does not mean you are only a victim in the story, or the only victim in it. It takes more than one person to make a relationship a success. It usually takes more than one person to cause a relationship to fail. In your case, one person decided to end it, but relationships often fail before they end. They can die long before they are pronounced dead and ultimately buried. The purpose of this entire book was to shed light on the things that can impact a relationship's future. Each partner has an obligation to guard against them, and none of us are ever totally careful with the things for which we are accountable. To take responsibility is not the same as accepting fault or blame. The breakup may not be your fault. It may be your ex-'s, or there could be no culprit at all. Accepting your part, though, helps to keep you from being a victim. Refusing to be a perpetual victim will help you heal, and healing is necessary to effectively move forward.

Finally, I want you rehabilitate your self-esteem. Rejection is a blow to the self-concept. Do not internalize the breakup in a manner that mars your view of yourself. Our relationship status should never be a key component of our self-esteem. You should not feel better about yourself because someone pursued you, and you should not feel worse because someone walked away. Your self-perception should never be influenced by the presence or absence of a romantic partner. You are who you are, the good, the bad, the ugly, and the beautiful. Trust what is good in you. Fix what is wrong with you. We all have to do the same. Remember your value, even if someone else discounts your worth. Do not allow the fact that a relationship ended damage, destroy, or deter you.

I'm sorry it ended. It is finished, but you are not. It is very cliché to say that endings create space for new beginnings, but it is none the less true. The new beginning that I speak of is not necessarily the beginning of a new relationship. That may not even be what you need most. I believe the most important new beginning after a relationship ends is a new healthy focus on one's self. Concentrate on yourself, not in an unhealthy narcissistic way, but in a way that seeks personal wholeness. Breakups can cause a brokenness of the soul. Seek to be whole prior to pursuing another relationship. Decide what type of person you want to take into the next phase of your life and into any future relationship. If it was a bad breakup or a bitter ending, it may take some time to get better. Take all the time you need. You will thank yourself later.

Conclusion

It has happened several times. After I have finished doing a talk on the subject of relationships, someone has approached me and asked the question, "Where were you 25 years ago?" Or, "Where were you before I got married?" Some have made this statement: "I needed you during my last relationship." While their queries and statements are meant to be complimentary, and I am grateful for their kindness, I see something deeper in what they say. I see personal reflection. Their questions and statements are indicative of intrapersonal contemplation and deliberation. Eventually, everyone reflects on their past relationships. It is natural and normal. We think about the breakups that were avoidable and those that were inevitable. We try to draw conclusions about what happened. We think about what we did and try to analyze what we did not or could not do. We remember the good times as well as relive the heartbreak and the frustration. While remembering some of our former romances, we ponder "what if?" With others, we emphatically declare, "I'm glad that's over." Relationships end. The only tragedy is when the end was avoidable.

It is my hope that you now understand the importance of consistently guarding the future of your relationship. We protect our unions by doing our best to create a positive relationship environment and behaving in a manner that does not sabotage the happy ending we so desire. There is one "end" that I did not talk about in the body of the book, and that is the end of time. I am certain that until the end of time, humanity will be trying to figure out how to make love relations work. I love seeing the happy older couples who seem to have found the answers. While I have attempted to delineate some principles and offer wisdom that I believe can be universally applied, love is ultimately an individual journey. I hope you have found or find that which is honorable, functional, and healthy for you, and since (or once) the right person has come along at the right moment, you keep loving together until the end of time.

46122684R00054

Made in the USA
Middletown, DE
24 May 2019